How Magic Tricks Work

Patrick Mangan

Harcourt Achieve

Rigby • Steck-Vaughn

www.HarcourtAchieve.com
1.800.531.5015

Rigby PM Extensions
Emerald

U.S. Edition © 2013 HMH Supplemental Publishers
10801 N. MoPac Expressway
Building #3
Austin, TX 78759
www.hmhsupplemental.com

Text © 2003 Cengage Learning Australia Pty Limited
Illustrations © 2003 Cengage Learning Australia Pty Limited
Originally published in Australia by Cengage Learning Australia

11   1957   17
4500676436

Text: Patrick Mangan
Printed in China by 1010 Printing International Ltd

Acknowledgments
The author and publisher would like to acknowledge permission to reproduce material from the following sources:
Photographs by Australian Picture Library/ Corbis, pp.8 left, 8 right/ AFP, p.12 right/ Bettmann, front page, pp.9 top, 20/ Corbis Sygma/ David Rose, pp.12 left, 13; Lindsay Edwards, back page, pp.4, 5, 6, 10 bottom, 11, 14, 15, 22; Imageaddict, p.10 top; Library of Congress/ McManus-Young Collection, p.9 bottom.

How Magic Tricks Work
ISBN 978 0 75 789211 0

Contents

Magic

Magic is exciting and mysterious, but many magic tricks are very simple to do. After reading this book you will be able to perform tricks that will have your friends scratching their heads in amazement!

To do these tricks, you will need some important magic equipment, and you will need to make your own **sliding box**.

Equipment needed:

rubber band

coins

bottle tops

toothpicks

an envelope

dice

cards

cards

a deck of cards

There are many ways to make your magic show more fun. Why not dress up as a magician or pretend to be an alien with magical powers? Use your imagination to think of outfits you could wear. You could even make a magician's hat out of cardboard or a colorful cape out of a sheet.

Don't worry if some of the tricks don't work very well the first time. Just keep practicing!

The Case of the Vanishing Toothpicks

The trick.

Shake the sliding box to show the audience that it is full of toothpicks.

But when you open it, the box is empty!

How to do it

- Make sure you are wearing a shirt with baggy sleeves.

- Attach a box full of toothpicks to your arm with rubber bands.

- When you shake the empty box, it will make a noise like it is full!

1. baggy shirt

2. toothpicks

3. rubber bands

4. shake shake shake rattle rattle

5. magic! it's empty!

The Houdini Files

Harry Houdini was one of the most famous magicians of all time. His real name was Ehrich Weiss. He was born in 1874 in Hungary, Europe. His family moved to America when he was four years old.

Houdini could escape from almost anything. He escaped from handcuffs, **leg irons**, coffins, and prison cells. He even escaped from a giant paper bag without tearing it!

His most famous trick was his underwater escape. He was locked in a wooden packing crate that was chained up and thrown into the sea. Houdini managed to escape but no one ever found out how he did it.

He practiced for this trick by holding his breath in a bathtub! He was able to hold his breath for nearly four minutes, which gave him more time to escape from the box.

As well as being a great magician, Houdini was also interested in flying planes. In 1910 he was the first person to fly a plane in Australia.

The Weeping Woman

The trick

Tell the audience you have a very magical coin. The face on the coin cries when you cover it. Cover the head of the coin with a closed fist and a couple of tears will fall from your hand. You were right!

How to do it

• Wet a small piece of tissue and roll it into a ball.

• Hide it between your fingers before you do the trick.

• Put the coin in your hand and squeeze hard. Water will drop from the wet tissue!

wet tissue

weeping coin!

The Money-making Box

The trick

Hold a sliding box halfway open and shake it to show the audience that it's empty. Drop a coin into the box and close it. When you open the box again, two coins are inside!

How to do it

- Balance another coin on the edge of the box tray.

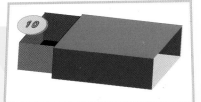

- Slowly push the tray into the box, but make sure that the coin is still stuck in place. Now you are ready to do the trick.

- Show a new coin to the audience and put it in the box.

- Then push the tray hard and your other coin will fall into the box as well. Presto, two coins!

Who is David Copperfield?

David Copperfield is a magician who performs his tricks on television. He is the richest and most famous magician in the world.

David started working as a magician when he was only 12 years old. When he was 16 years old, he taught magic at New York University!

He can do many unbelievable tricks. He has performed several of these tricks during his TV specials. Once he flew high above the audience and it was impossible to tell how he stayed up in the air. Another incredible trick involved him walking straight through the **Great Wall of China!**

Perhaps the most brilliant trick he has performed was in New York. He made the Statue of Liberty disappear!

Kings in a Hurry

The trick

Get an audience member to shuffle a deck of cards and hand them back to you. Tell the audience that kings expect special treatment – they make sure they are always at the top. Put the deck of cards behind your back and take out the top four cards one by one. As you predicted, they are all kings!

How to do it

- You will need a back pocket to do this trick.

- Before the trick, take out all four kings and put them in your back pocket.

- When the deck of cards is returned from the audience, put the cards behind your back.

- Take the four kings out of your pocket and put them on top of the deck.

- Show the deck of cards to the audience again. Take four cards off the top of the deck one by one. They are all kings!

4 kings!

The Pushy Card

The trick

Show the audience the top card from a deck and put it back. Then put the top card at the bottom of the deck. Tap the card three times and tell the audience it has pushed its way back to the top. Show them the top card, and they won't believe their eyes!

How to do it

- When you pick up the top card to show to the audience, you actually pick up the top two cards. The audience is really seeing the second card.

- The card you put at the bottom of the deck is not the card the audience has seen. The card they have seen is still at the top of the deck.

- When you tap the cards, pretend it's hard work to make the card go back to the top. But only you know it's already there!

Magical Horses

Throughout history there have been many amazing animals that people have told stories about. Some of these stories have been about horses with magical powers.

The **unicorn** was a horse with a single horn in the middle of its forehead. Drinking from the horn of a unicorn was supposed to protect you from poison. A crushed horn was thought to cure many diseases.

Unicorns were impossible to catch because they moved so fast. The best thing to do was to trick them into getting their horn stuck in a tree.

Unicorns Beware

There was another famous horse called Pegasus, from **Greek mythology**. Pegasus was a beautiful white horse with golden wings.

A young warrior named Bellerophon, in Greek mythology, flew off on Pegasus looking for adventure. He killed a fire-breathing dragon and a tribe of other warriors. Bellerophon went too far and tried to fly to heaven on Pegasus. Zeus, the king of the gods in Greek mythology, sent an insect to tickle the magic horse and throw Bellerophon off. Pegasus flew up to heaven and turned into a **constellation** of stars. The stars are still up there in the sky today.

The Obedient Dice

The trick

Give a sealed envelope to a member of the audience. Then put two dice into a sliding box and shake it. Tell the audience you're going to tell the dice which numbers to show. Pretend to whisper something to the dice. Tell the audience the numbers on the dice will be the same as the numbers on the piece of paper inside the envelope. Open the box to show the numbers on the dice, and then open the envelope. You were right!

How to do it

2 dice
stuck down

- Before you do the trick, stick two dice to the bottom of the tray at one end of the box.

- Write down the numbers you see on the top of the dice on a piece of paper and put it in the envelope.

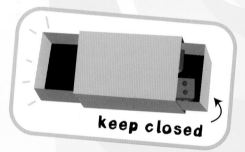

keep closed

- When you open the box in front of the audience to put the other dice inside, make sure you don't open the end with the dice stuck to the bottom!

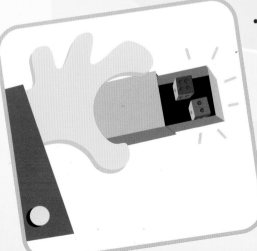

- After you've shaken the box, carefully open it showing the audience the end of the box that has the dice stuck down.

19

Ventriloquists

Ventriloquists aren't exactly magicians, but they certainly seem magical. Ventriloquists can make puppets look like they are actually talking. A really good ventriloquist makes you believe the puppets are alive!

There is one difficult thing about being a ventriloquist. You have to be able to talk without moving your lips. This is how you make it appear that the puppet can talk.

Try it yourself. It's not easy, is it?

I'm hungry!

The word ventriloquist means "belly speaker," in the old language of **Latin**. Over two thousand years ago, it was believed that special people called **prophets** could talk to the spirits of the dead. People thought these spirits lived in the stomachs of the prophets.

People didn't realize that these prophets had discovered how to talk without moving their lips. They could make people think the voices were really coming from their stomachs.

These prophets were the world's first ventriloquists!

X-ray Vision

The trick

This trick will prove that you have x-ray vision! Put three bottle tops on a table. Then give a coin to someone in the audience and ask them to put it under one of the tops, without you looking. Everyone will be surprised when you can tell them where the coin is hidden. It's incredible what you can do with x-ray vision!

How to do it

• The trick is all in your head. Actually, it's all on your head.

• You need a hair for this trick, about 1 inch long.

• Glue the hair to the coin. You will be able to see the hidden coin because the hair will be sticking out from under the bottle top!

NEWS FLASH!

Nine-year-old girl is the world's magic expert

A nine-year-old girl claims to be the world's number one expert on fantastical facts and fantastical creatures. "It's true," said Hazel. "I know everything there is to know about fantasy!

Did you know that **Merlin the Magician** made **Stonehenge** move from Ireland to England, hundreds of years ago?"

Hazel kept talking. "And did you realize that **leprechauns** keep their gold in a pottery jar? And did you know that they are shoe-makers?"

Teachers at Hazel's school are worried about her. "Children need to be interested in subjects other than fantasy," said one teacher.

Meanwhile, Hazel just kept talking about fantasies. "Did you know that some **fairies** can't stand the sound of bells?" she said.

"And do you know how to make time fly?" she asked the other children in her class.

No one replied, because everyone already knew how to make time fly. Just throw a clock out of the window.

Glossary

constellation   a group of stars in the sky that look like a certain shape

fairies   tiny make-believe people who can help or hurt humans

Great Wall of China   a huge stone wall almost 4,000 miles long standing in the mountains of China, built thousands of years ago

Greek mythology   stories out of Greece from ancient times

Latin   the language of ancient Rome

leg irons   metal cuffs attached with chains that can be placed around a person's leg

Merlin the Magician   a fantastical character in stories from Old Britain

prophets   people who are believed to have special powers in communicating with spirits

sliding box   an open-topped box that fits into a box sleeve and is used in tricks

Stonehenge   a group of very tall rocks freestanding in England

unicorn   an imaginary horse with one horn on its forehead

Ventriloquists   people who can talk clearly from their throat without moving their mouths